UNDERSTANDING BORDERLINE PERSONALITY DISORDER

Comprehensive Guide To Symptoms, Treatment, And Managing Emotional Instability

DR. LINCOLN WAYLON

DISCLAIMER

This book contains information that should only be used for educational and informational reasons; it is not meant to be used as a source of medical or psychological advice. The author's studies, life experiences, and expertise in the area of health and wellness served as the foundation for the content. It should not, however, be used in place of expert counsel, a diagnosis, or medical care.

Any queries you may have about a physical or mental health issue should always be directed toward the advice of a licensed healthcare provider or mental health specialist. With regard to the efficacy or outcomes of the methods or suggestions included in this book, the author and publisher make no representations or warranties.

Any information or methods in this book are used entirely at the reader's own risk and discretion. The material provided here may be used or misused, and neither the author nor the publisher will be held responsible for any results, losses, or negative impacts.

Keep in mind that everyone has different demands and reactions to health and wellness routines. Any health and wellness plans you implement must be customized to your particular circumstances, and you should speak with experts to make sure the plans meet your needs.

TABLE OF CONTENTS

ABOUT THE BOOK

"Understanding Borderline Personality Disorder" serves as a crucial resource for both individuals and professionals seeking to grasp the complexities of this challenging condition. Borderline Personality Disorder (BPD) is characterized by emotional instability, impulsive behaviors, distorted self-image, and turbulent relationships, all of which can significantly impact one's daily life and interpersonal dynamics. By offering a comprehensive overview, this book provides clarity on the definition and key characteristics of BPD, tracing its historical evolution and presenting up-to-date prevalence statistics. The emphasis on accurate diagnosis underscores the importance of distinguishing BPD from other mental health conditions, utilizing DSM-5 criteria, and employing various assessment tools and techniques.

Understanding the core symptoms of BPD—such as emotional instability, impulsivity, and chronic feelings of emptiness—is essential for effective treatment and management.

The book delves into these symptoms in detail, exploring their impact on individuals' lives and relationships. Additionally, the discussion on the causes and risk factors of BPD provides insight into genetic predispositions, childhood trauma, neurobiological factors, and environmental influences, highlighting how these elements interact to contribute to the disorder's development.

Treatment approaches for BPD are explored in depth, offering an overview of Cognitive Behavioral Therapy (CBT), Dialectical Behavior Therapy (DBT), and medication options.

The book also discusses integrative treatment approaches that combine various therapeutic modalities to address the multifaceted nature of BPD. Self-help strategies are emphasized, including mindfulness and relaxation techniques, building healthy habits, and utilizing support networks. These resources are crucial for individuals seeking to manage their symptoms and improve their quality of life.

Navigating relationships with BPD poses unique challenges, and the book provides practical strategies for managing romantic relationships, family dynamics, and workplace interactions. It also addresses the importance of healthy communication, setting boundaries, and maintaining expectations to foster supportive and functional relationships.

Crisis management and safety planning are integral aspects of dealing with BPD. The book offers guidance on identifying warning signs, developing a crisis plan, seeking emergency help, and implementing safety techniques. Support resources for crises are also discussed, ensuring that individuals have access to the necessary help during critical times.

Long-term management and recovery are pivotal to achieving sustained improvement and stability. The book outlines methods for setting and achieving personal goals, monitoring progress, and addressing setbacks.

Emphasis is placed on building a supportive environment and encouraging ongoing therapy and support to foster recovery and personal development.

The book addresses common concerns and provides detailed FAQs about BPD, including its diagnosis, treatment options, symptom management, and available resources. This comprehensive approach ensures that readers have access to valuable information and practical advice to better understand and manage Borderline Personality Disorder.

CHAPTER ONE

OVERVIEW OF BORDERLINE PERSONALITY DISORDER

DEFINITION AND KEY CHARACTERISTICS

Borderline Personality Disorder (BPD) is a complex mental health condition marked by pervasive instability in moods, self-image, and interpersonal relationships. Individuals with BPD often experience intense and fluctuating emotions, leading to significant challenges in managing relationships and self-identity. Key characteristics include chronic feelings of emptiness, fear of abandonment, and impulsive behaviors that can lead to self-harm or suicidal actions. Emotional instability is a core feature, with rapid mood changes that can be triggered by external events or internal conflicts.

In addition to emotional instability, people with BPD may exhibit a pattern of unstable and intense interpersonal relationships, where idealization can quickly shift to devaluation.

They often struggle with a distorted self-image, leading to a sense of identity confusion and instability. Impulsive behaviors, such as spending sprees, substance abuse, or risky sexual activities, are common and can exacerbate interpersonal conflicts and self-esteem issues. Recognizing these characteristics is crucial for understanding the challenges faced by individuals with BPD.

HISTORICAL CONTEXT AND EVOLUTION

The concept of Borderline Personality Disorder emerged in the mid-20th century as mental health professionals began to recognize a pattern of symptoms that did not fit neatly into existing diagnostic categories.

Initially, BPD was described as a borderline state between neurosis and psychosis, reflecting its complex and often puzzling nature. Early theories suggested that BPD might result from severe emotional instability or early childhood trauma, but the understanding was limited.

Over the decades, the definition and understanding of BPD have evolved significantly. Advances in psychological research and clinical practice have led to a more nuanced view of the disorder, incorporating biological, psychological, and social factors. Contemporary perspectives emphasize the role of genetic predisposition and early-life experiences in shaping the development of BPD. The evolution of diagnostic criteria in the DSM (Diagnostic and Statistical Manual of Mental Disorders) has refined the understanding of BPD, providing a clearer framework for diagnosis and treatment.

PREVALENCE AND STATISTICAL DATA

Research indicates that Borderline Personality Disorder affects approximately 1.6% of the general population, though prevalence rates can vary based on the population studied and diagnostic criteria used. BPD is more commonly diagnosed in women, with estimates suggesting that about 75% of those diagnosed are female.

However, it is important to note that BPD can occur in individuals of any gender and across various demographic groups.

The prevalence of BPD also varies in different settings. In clinical populations, such as that receiving mental health treatment, the rate of BPD diagnoses can be significantly higher, sometimes exceeding 10%. Understanding these prevalence rates helps in recognizing the extent of the disorder and the importance of addressing it within mental health services. Accurate data on BPD prevalence is crucial for planning effective treatment and support services.

IMPORTANCE OF ACCURATE DIAGNOSIS

Accurate diagnosis of Borderline Personality Disorder is essential for effective treatment and management. Misdiagnosis can lead to inappropriate treatment plans and exacerbate the symptoms of BPD. The complexity of BPD symptoms, which often overlap with other mental health disorders such as mood disorders, anxiety disorders, and post-traumatic stress disorder (PTSD), requires careful and comprehensive assessment by a qualified mental health professional.

An accurate diagnosis involves a thorough evaluation, including a detailed clinical interview, assessment of symptom patterns, and consideration of the individual's history. Tools such as structured interviews and diagnostic questionnaires can aid in distinguishing BPD from other conditions. Early and precise diagnosis allows for timely intervention, which can significantly improve outcomes and quality of life for individuals with BPD.

OVERVIEW OF TREATMENT APPROACHES

Treatment for Borderline Personality Disorder typically involves a combination of psychotherapy, medication, and support services. Psychotherapy, particularly Dialectical Behavior Therapy (DBT) and Cognitive Behavioral Therapy (CBT) is considered the cornerstone of treatment. DBT focuses on helping individuals develop coping skills to manage emotional instability and reduce self-harm behaviors. CBT aims to address negative thought patterns and improve emotional regulation.

Medications may be prescribed to manage co-occurring symptoms such as depression, anxiety, or impulsivity, although there is no specific medication for BPD itself. Support services, including peer support groups and psychoeducation, can provide additional help in managing symptoms and improving quality of life. An integrated approach that combines these treatment modalities can offer a comprehensive strategy for managing BPD and enhancing overall well-being.

CHAPTER TWO

CORE SYMPTOMS OF BPD

EMOTIONAL INSTABILITY

Emotional instability in Borderline Personality Disorder (BPD) is characterized by rapid and intense shifts in mood. Individuals with BPD may experience frequent mood swings, such as going from feeling happy and excited to deeply sad or irritable within a short period.

This emotional turbulence is often triggered by stress or interpersonal conflicts and can significantly affect daily functioning and relationships.

To manage emotional instability, it's crucial to develop emotional regulation skills. Techniques such as mindfulness, cognitive restructuring, and distress tolerance can help individuals recognize and manage their emotional responses more effectively. Practicing mindfulness involves paying attention to the present moment without judgment, which can help in observing emotional shifts without being overwhelmed by them.

Additionally, seeking therapy, particularly Dialectical Behavior Therapy (DBT), can be highly beneficial. DBT focuses on providing skills to manage emotions, improve interpersonal effectiveness, and build a more stable sense of self. Working with a mental health professional can provide guidance and support in developing these crucial skills for emotional stability.

IMPULSIVE BEHAVIORS

Impulsive behaviors are a hallmark of BPD and can manifest as sudden, risky actions without considering the consequences. This might include spending sprees, substance abuse, reckless driving, or self-harm. Impulsivity can stem from intense emotional states and can lead to significant personal and social difficulties.

To address impulsive behaviors, developing coping strategies is essential.

Techniques such as identifying triggers for impulsivity, using mindfulness to increase awareness of urges, and employing behavioral interventions can be effective. For example, creating a list of alternative activities or distractions can help divert attention from impulsive urges.

Engaging in structured activities and setting clear, achievable goals can also reduce the likelihood of impulsive actions. Therapy, especially DBT, often includes modules specifically designed to manage impulsivity and improve decision-making skills. Working with a therapist can help individuals develop practical strategies to control and redirect impulsive tendencies.

DISTORTED SELF-IMAGE

A distorted self-image in BPD involves an unstable or distorted sense of self. Individuals may have conflicting feelings about their identity, leading to feelings of worthlessness or inadequacy. This unstable self-concept can contribute to difficulties in forming and maintaining relationships and achieving personal goals.

To address a distorted self-image, it's important to work on self-awareness and self-acceptance. Techniques such as self-reflection, journaling, and therapy can aid in developing a more stable sense of self. Cognitive-behavioral approaches can help challenge and reframe negative self-beliefs and replace them with more balanced and positive views.

Therapy can play a crucial role in helping individuals understand and stabilize their self-image. Therapies such as DBT or psychodynamic therapy focus on exploring and understanding the underlying factors contributing to a distorted self-image and working towards developing a more cohesive and positive self-concept.

INTENSE AND UNSTABLE RELATIONSHIPS

People with BPD often experience intense and unstable relationships characterized by extremes of idealization and devaluation. Relationships may start with intense closeness but can quickly shift to feelings of betrayal or disappointment. This instability can lead to frequent conflicts and challenges in maintaining healthy, lasting relationships.

Managing relationship instability involves improving interpersonal skills and communication. Learning to recognize and address patterns of idealization and devaluation is key. Techniques such as assertiveness training and relationship-focused therapy can help individuals communicate their needs more effectively and build healthier relationship patterns.

Therapeutic interventions, particularly DBT, offer strategies for improving interpersonal effectiveness. These include skills for managing conflict, setting boundaries, and fostering healthy connections. Working with a therapist can provide support in developing and practicing these skills to achieve more stable and fulfilling relationships.

Chronic feelings of emptiness in BPD are marked by a pervasive sense of inner void or lack of fulfillment. Individuals may feel as though they have no purpose or direction, which can lead to a constant search for external validation or stimulation to fill this void. This sensation can significantly impact their overall well-being and satisfaction with life.

Addressing feelings of emptiness involves finding meaningful and fulfilling activities and goals. Engaging in hobbies, setting personal goals, and participating in activities that bring joy and satisfaction can help counteract these feelings. Exploring and pursuing personal interests can provide a sense of purpose and direction.

CHAPTER THREE

DIAGNOSTIC CRITERIA FOR BPD

DSM-5 CRITERIA

Borderline Personality Disorder (BPD) is characterized by a pattern of instability in interpersonal relationships, self-image, and affect, coupled with marked impulsivity. The DSM-5 outlines specific criteria for diagnosing BPD, including a pervasive pattern of instability in self-image, mood, and interpersonal relationships. This instability is reflected through symptoms such as frantic efforts to avoid real or imagined abandonment, unstable and intense interpersonal relationships, and identity disturbance. Individuals often exhibit impulsive behaviors in areas like spending, sex, substance abuse, and reckless driving. To meet the criteria, the individual must demonstrate at least five of these symptoms, which must cause significant distress or impairment in social, occupational, or other important areas of functioning.

A critical aspect of DSM-5 diagnosis involves evaluating the duration and intensity of symptoms. For a diagnosis of BPD, symptoms must be persistent over a long period, typically beginning in early adulthood. The criteria require that symptoms are not better explained by another mental disorder or due to substance abuse or a medical condition. Additionally, the DSM-5 emphasizes the necessity of a comprehensive clinical interview and history-taking to confirm that the symptoms are consistent with BPD and not attributable to transient emotional responses or other conditions.

Practically, diagnosing BPD using DSM-5 criteria involves a structured assessment process. Clinicians use specific diagnostic interviews and self-report questionnaires to gather data on the patient's symptoms and their impact on daily life. The information collected must be carefully analyzed in the context of the DSM-5 criteria to ensure an accurate diagnosis. This process involves ruling out other mental health conditions with similar symptoms and confirming that the symptomatology aligns with the BPD criteria as outlined in the DSM-5.

ASSESSMENT TOOLS AND TECHNIQUES

Assessment tools for Borderline Personality Disorder (BPD) include structured interviews, self-report questionnaires, and behavioral assessments. One commonly used tool is the Structured Clinical Interview for DSM-5 (SCID-5), which provides a detailed framework for assessing BPD symptoms through a standardized approach. The SCID-5 helps clinicians systematically evaluate the presence and severity of BPD symptoms based on DSM-5 criteria. This structured interview is designed to elicit information about the patient's interpersonal relationships, emotional regulation, and behavioral patterns, providing a comprehensive assessment of their mental health status.

Self-report questionnaires, such as the Borderline Evaluation of Severity Over Time (BEST) and the McLean Screening Instrument for Borderline

Personality Disorder (MSI-BPD), are also essential tools. These instruments allow individuals to self-report their symptoms and experiences, offering insights into their internal emotional states and behavioral tendencies.

Self-report measures can be particularly useful for tracking changes in symptom severity over time and evaluating the effectiveness of therapeutic interventions.

Behavioral assessments involve observing the individual's interactions and behaviors in various settings, such as therapy sessions or daily life. This approach helps clinicians understand how symptoms manifest in real-world contexts and assess the impact of symptoms on the individual's functioning. Combining these assessment tools provides a multifaceted view of the individual's symptoms and helps guide the development of an effective treatment plan tailored to their specific needs.

Differentiating Borderline Personality Disorder (BPD) from other mental health conditions is crucial for accurate diagnosis and effective treatment. BPD shares symptoms with several other disorders, including mood disorders, anxiety disorders, and other personality disorders.

For instance, the emotional instability and interpersonal difficulties seen in BPD can overlap with symptoms of bipolar disorder and major depressive disorder. However, BPD is characterized by its pervasive pattern of instability across multiple domains, including self-image and relationships, which is less common in mood disorders.

Another challenge is distinguishing BPD from other personality disorders, such as narcissistic personality disorder or histrionic personality disorder. While BPD involves instability in self-image and intense emotional responses, narcissistic and histrionic personality disorders are marked by different patterns of behavior, such as grandiosity in narcissism and attention-seeking in histrionics. Clinicians must carefully assess the presence and consistency of symptoms across different contexts to differentiate BPD from these other disorders accurately.

Additionally, substance use disorders and trauma-related disorders, like post-traumatic stress disorder (PTSD), can present with symptoms similar to those of BPD. Substance abuse can exacerbate emotional instability and impulsive behavior, while PTSD may involve emotional dysregulation and interpersonal difficulties.

Accurate diagnosis involves a thorough assessment of the individual's history and current symptomatology to ensure that symptoms are not solely attributable to substance use or trauma, thereby distinguishing BPD from these conditions.

Mental health professionals play a critical role in diagnosing and treating Borderline Personality Disorder (BPD). Psychiatrists and clinical psychologists are typically involved in diagnosing BPD using DSM-5 criteria and assessment tools. They conduct comprehensive evaluations to determine the presence of BPD symptoms and their impact on the individual's functioning. Psychiatrists may also prescribe medication to manage co-occurring conditions such as depression or anxiety, while psychologists often provide psychotherapy to address the core symptoms of BPD.

Therapists specializing in Dialectical Behavior Therapy (DBT) and other evidence-based therapies are essential in the treatment of BPD. DBT, developed specifically for BPD, focuses on helping individuals develop skills for emotional regulation, interpersonal effectiveness, and distress tolerance. Therapists work with patients to build coping strategies, improve interpersonal relationships, and manage self-destructive behaviors. The therapeutic process is highly collaborative, involving both individual therapy and group sessions to address various aspects of the disorder.

Social workers and counselors may also be involved in supporting individuals with BPD. They provide case management, connect clients with community resources, and offer support in navigating daily life challenges. Social workers often play a key role in advocating for patients, ensuring they receive appropriate care, and assisting with issues such as housing, employment, and social support. Their work complements the efforts of psychiatrists and therapists in addressing the multifaceted needs of individuals with BPD.

CHALLENGES IN DIAGNOSIS

Diagnosing Borderline Personality Disorder (BPD) presents several challenges, primarily due to the complexity and variability of symptoms.

The overlapping nature of BPD symptoms with those of other mental health conditions can complicate the diagnostic process. Clinicians must carefully differentiate BPD from other disorders with similar presentations, such as mood disorders or substance abuse disorders. This requires a thorough assessment and often a longitudinal evaluation to observe symptom patterns over time.

Another challenge is the stigma associated with BPD, which can affect both diagnosis and treatment. Individuals with BPD may experience negative attitudes from healthcare providers or face difficulties accessing appropriate care due to misconceptions about the disorder. Stigma can also impact the individual's willingness to seek help and engage in treatment, further complicating the diagnostic and therapeutic process.

Finally, the dynamic nature of BPD symptoms adds to the diagnostic challenges. Symptoms of BPD can fluctuate significantly, making it difficult to capture a stable picture of the individual's condition.

Clinicians must rely on detailed assessments, including comprehensive clinical interviews and standardized questionnaires, to obtain an accurate understanding of the individual's symptoms and their impact on daily functioning. This thorough approach is essential for making an accurate diagnosis and developing an effective treatment plan.

CHAPTER FOUR

UNDERSTANDING THE CAUSES AND RISK FACTORS

GENETIC PREDISPOSITIONS

Borderline Personality Disorder (BPD) has been linked to genetic factors, suggesting that those with a family history of the disorder may be at a higher risk. Genetic predispositions can affect brain function and emotional regulation, influencing the development of BPD. Researchers have identified specific genetic markers and variations that may contribute to the disorder's onset, though no single gene is responsible. Understanding these genetic links can help in identifying individuals who may benefit from early intervention and support.

When examining genetic predispositions, it's essential to consider both the hereditary and environmental components. Family studies have shown that BPD can run in families, indicating a possible genetic influence.

However, the presence of genetic markers alone does not determine whether an individual will develop BPD; it simply increases the likelihood. Genetics interact with various environmental factors, making it crucial to consider the broader context in which these genetic predispositions manifest.

Identifying genetic risk factors involves analyzing family history and conducting genetic testing, which can provide insights into an individual's vulnerability to BPD. This information can guide preventive measures and therapeutic approaches. However, genetic predispositions are only one piece of the puzzle, and a comprehensive evaluation of all risk factors is necessary for a complete understanding of BPD.

IMPACT OF CHILDHOOD TRAUMA

Childhood trauma is a significant risk factor for Borderline Personality Disorder. Experiences such as physical, emotional, or sexual abuse, as well as neglect, can profoundly impact a child's emotional development and sense of self. Trauma can disrupt the formation of healthy attachments and coping mechanisms, leading to difficulties in emotional regulation and interpersonal relationships later in life.

Traumatic experiences during critical developmental periods can shape how individuals perceive themselves and others. Children who experience trauma may develop maladaptive coping strategies and a distorted sense of self-worth, which are characteristic of BPD.

Addressing past trauma through therapeutic approaches like trauma-focused therapy can be crucial in managing symptoms and promoting emotional healing.

In therapy, it is essential to create a safe and supportive environment where individuals can process their trauma. Techniques such as cognitive-behavioral therapy (CBT) and dialectical behavior therapy (DBT) are often used to help individuals understand and work through their past experiences. Acknowledging and addressing childhood trauma can significantly contribute to the overall treatment and management of BPD.

NEUROBIOLOGICAL FACTORS

Neurobiological factors play a crucial role in the development of Borderline Personality Disorder. Research has shown that abnormalities in brain structure and function, particularly in areas related to emotion regulation, impulse control, and self-identity, are associated with BPD. The amygdala, prefrontal cortex, and hippocampus are among the brain regions implicated in BPD, reflecting how these areas contribute to emotional instability and interpersonal difficulties.

Neurobiological studies have also highlighted the role of neurotransmitters and hormonal imbalances in BPD. For example, dysregulation in the serotonin and dopamine systems has been linked to mood instability and impulsive behaviors.

Understanding these biological underpinnings can inform treatment strategies, such as medication management and neurobiological interventions, to address specific symptoms associated with BPD.

Treatment plans often include a combination of medication and psychotherapy to address neurobiological factors. Medications that target neurotransmitter imbalances can help stabilize mood and reduce impulsivity. Additionally, integrating neurobiological insights with therapeutic techniques can enhance treatment efficacy and support individuals in managing their symptoms more effectively.

ENVIRONMENTAL INFLUENCES

Environmental influences significantly contribute to the development of Borderline Personality Disorder. Factors such as unstable family environments, chronic stress, and exposure to substance abuse can create conditions that increase the risk of developing BPD.

A chaotic or neglectful environment during formative years can impact emotional stability and interpersonal skills, which are critical components of BPD.

Positive environmental factors, such as supportive relationships and stable home environments, can mitigate some of the risks associated with BPD. Creating a nurturing and stable environment is essential for emotional development and resilience. Therapeutic interventions often focus on improving the individual's environmental context by fostering supportive relationships and reducing exposure to stressors.

Interventions that address environmental influences involve creating stability and predictability in daily life. Support from family, friends, and mental health professionals can help individuals build coping skills and establish a healthier emotional foundation. By addressing and modifying adverse environmental factors, individuals with BPD can experience significant improvements in their overall well-being.

The interaction of risk factors in Borderline Personality Disorder is complex, as genetic predispositions, childhood trauma, neurobiological factors, and environmental influences often intersect. These factors do not operate in isolation; rather, they interact in ways that can exacerbate or mitigate the risk of developing BPD.

For instance, a person with a genetic predisposition may be more vulnerable to the effects of childhood trauma or environmental stressors.

Understanding how these risk factors interact helps in developing a comprehensive treatment plan. It involves assessing the interplay between biological, psychological, and environmental factors to identify how they contribute to the individual's symptoms. Tailoring treatment to address these interactions can improve outcomes and support effective management of BPD.

A holistic approach that considers the interaction of multiple risk factors is essential for effective treatment. Integrating strategies that address genetic, traumatic, neurobiological, and environmental components can lead to more personalized and effective interventions. By recognizing and addressing the complex interplay of risk factors, individuals with BPD can achieve better symptom management and overall quality of life.

CHAPTER FIVE

TREATMENT APPROACHES FOR BPD

COGNITIVE BEHAVIORAL THERAPY (CBT)

Cognitive Behavioral Therapy (CBT) is a widely used treatment for Borderline Personality Disorder (BPD) that focuses on identifying and altering negative thought patterns and behaviors. The therapy involves working with a trained therapist to recognize distorted thinking and learn practical skills to manage emotional responses. Clients are encouraged to challenge their irrational beliefs and replace them with more balanced and realistic thoughts. This process helps in reducing symptoms like impulsivity and emotional instability by fostering healthier ways of thinking and behaving.

In CBT, therapy sessions typically involve exercises such as cognitive restructuring, where individuals practice changing their negative thought patterns. Behavioral experiments may also be used to test the validity of these thoughts and observe the outcomes of new behaviors. Clients might be assigned homework tasks to practice these new skills in real-life situations, such as keeping a thought diary or engaging in positive activities. This hands-on approach ensures that individuals actively apply what they learn in therapy to their daily lives.

Furthermore, CBT aims to build coping strategies for managing stress and difficult emotions. Techniques such as problem-solving and relaxation training are integrated into the therapy to equip individuals with tools to handle emotional crises more effectively. By combining cognitive restructuring with practical coping mechanisms, CBT provides a structured approach to improving emotional regulation and reducing BPD symptoms.

DIALECTICAL BEHAVIOR THERAPY (DBT)

Dialectical Behavior Therapy (DBT) is specifically designed for individuals with BPD, focusing on balancing acceptance with change.

DBT combines cognitive-behavioral techniques with mindfulness practices to help clients develop skills for managing intense emotions and improving interpersonal relationships. The therapy emphasizes the importance of accepting oneself while simultaneously working towards personal growth and change, thus addressing the core struggles of BPD.

DBT includes four primary skill areas: mindfulness, distress tolerance, emotion regulation, and interpersonal effectiveness. Mindfulness teaches individuals to be present and fully aware of their experiences without judgment, which helps in managing emotional responses. Distress tolerance skills provide techniques for coping with crises without resorting to harmful behaviors, while emotion regulation skills focus on understanding and modulating intense emotions. Interpersonal effectiveness training helps clients build healthier relationships by improving communication and assertiveness.

Therapy often involves individual sessions and group skills training. In individual therapy, clients work one-on-one with a therapist to apply DBT skills to their specific challenges, while group sessions offer peer support and practice of the skills learned. This combination of individual and group work ensures comprehensive support and skill development for managing BPD symptoms effectively.

MEDICATION OPTIONS

Medication can be an important component in the treatment of BPD, particularly for managing co-occurring conditions like depression, anxiety, or mood disorders. While no medication is specifically approved for BPD, several types can help alleviate symptoms and improve overall functioning. Antidepressants, such as selective serotonin reuptake inhibitors (SSRIs), can help with mood stabilization and reduce symptoms of depression and anxiety.

Mood stabilizers, such as lithium or valproic acid, may be prescribed to help manage mood swings and impulsive behavior. Additionally, atypical antipsychotics can be used to address symptoms like paranoia or severe mood disturbances. Individuals must work closely with their healthcare provider to find the most effective medication regimen, as responses to medications can vary.

Medication management often involves regular follow-up appointments to monitor effectiveness and adjust dosages as needed. Individuals should be aware of potential side effects and communicate any concerns with their healthcare provider. Medication is typically used in conjunction with therapy to provide a comprehensive treatment approach for managing BPD.

INTEGRATIVE TREATMENT APPROACHES

Integrative treatment approaches for BPD combine various therapeutic modalities to address the complex needs of individuals. This approach may include blending CBT, DBT, and medication with other therapeutic practices to create a personalized treatment plan. The goal is to address multiple facets of BPD symptoms through a tailored and holistic approach, incorporating different strategies to enhance overall well-being.

For instance, integrating mindfulness practices with cognitive and behavioral techniques can help clients develop a well-rounded set of skills for managing their emotions and improving their relationships. This might involve combining DBT's focus on mindfulness with CBT's cognitive restructuring to offer a more comprehensive skill set. Additionally, incorporating support from other mental health professionals, such as family therapists or occupational therapists, can provide additional perspectives and strategies.

Regular evaluations and adjustments to the treatment plan ensure that the integrated approach remains effective. By combining different therapeutic methods and considering the individual's unique needs, integrative approaches aim to offer a more flexible and comprehensive treatment strategy for BPD.

BENEFITS OF THERAPY AND MEDICATION

The combination of therapy and medication offers significant benefits for individuals with BPD. Therapy provides a structured framework for understanding and managing symptoms, developing coping strategies, and improving interpersonal skills. Cognitive Behavioral Therapy (CBT) and Dialectical Behavior Therapy (DBT) both offer evidence-based approaches for addressing the emotional and behavioral challenges of BPD, promoting lasting change and emotional stability.

Medication, while not a standalone treatment, can complement therapy by addressing underlying mood disorders or severe symptoms. By managing co-occurring conditions and stabilizing mood, medication can enhance the effectiveness of therapeutic interventions. Together, therapy and medication can lead to improved emotional regulation, better relationships, and an overall enhanced quality of life for individuals with BPD.

The collaborative nature of therapy and medication provides a multifaceted approach to treatment, allowing individuals to benefit from both psychological support and pharmacological management. This comprehensive approach helps address the diverse aspects of BPD, leading to more effective symptom control and a greater ability to achieve personal and therapeutic goals.

CHAPTER SIX

SELF-HELP STRATEGIES AND RESOURCES

MINDFULNESS AND RELAXATION TECHNIQUES

Mindfulness and relaxation techniques are essential tools for managing Borderline Personality Disorder (BPD). Practicing mindfulness involves paying full attention to the present moment without judgment, which helps individuals become more aware of their thoughts and emotions. Techniques such as deep breathing, progressive muscle relaxation, and guided imagery can significantly reduce stress and anxiety. By focusing on the present, individuals can gain better control over their emotional responses and develop a sense of calm amidst the chaos of their emotions.

To effectively integrate mindfulness into daily life, individuals can start by setting aside a few minutes each day for mindfulness practice. Techniques such as mindful breathing or body scans can be incorporated into routines to help manage overwhelming emotions. Apps and online resources offer guided sessions that can be helpful for beginners, providing step-by-step instructions and support as they learn to focus on the present moment and relax their minds and body.

Relaxation techniques, such as progressive muscle relaxation, help to reduce physical tension that often accompanies emotional stress. By systematically tensing and then relaxing different muscle groups, individuals can release built-up tension and promote a greater sense of physical and emotional ease. Regular practice of these techniques can improve overall well-being and enhance the ability to cope with stressors related to BPD.

BUILDING HEALTHY HABITS

Building healthy habits is crucial for managing Borderline Personality Disorder and promoting overall well-being. Establishing a routine that includes regular exercise, balanced nutrition, and adequate sleep helps stabilize mood and enhance emotional resilience. Exercise releases endorphins, which can improve mood and reduce symptoms of anxiety and depression. A balanced diet supports physical health, which in turn supports mental health, and sufficient sleep is essential for emotional regulation.

Creating a structured daily routine can also help individuals with BPD maintain stability and predictability in their lives. This involves setting specific times for meals, exercise, work, and relaxation.

Developing a consistent routine helps to minimize feelings of chaos and unpredictability, which can trigger emotional distress? Small, manageable changes, such as setting a regular bedtime or planning meals, can contribute to a more stable and balanced life.

Incorporating self-care activities into daily routines, such as journaling, hobbies, or relaxation exercises, supports emotional well-being and personal growth. These activities provide opportunities for individuals to engage in positive, fulfilling experiences that counterbalance the stressors associated with BPD. Regularly setting aside time for self-care helps individuals maintain a sense of control and fosters a more positive outlook.

<h2 style="text-align:center">UTILIZING SUPPORT NETWORKS</h2>

Utilizing support networks is vital for individuals with Borderline Personality Disorder as it provides a sense of connection and reduces feelings of isolation. Support networks can include family, friends, mental health professionals, and support groups. Engaging with supportive individuals who understand the challenges of BPD can offer encouragement, validation, and practical advice, which can significantly aid in managing symptoms and improving quality of life.

Support groups, both in-person and online, offer a platform for individuals with BPD to share experiences and coping strategies with others facing similar challenges. These groups provide a safe space for discussing emotions and receiving feedback from peers who have a deep understanding of the disorder. Finding a group that fits one's needs and comfort level can be an invaluable resource for gaining insights and building a sense of community.

Mental health professionals, such as therapists and counselors, play a crucial role in providing specialized support and guidance. They can help individuals develop coping strategies, work through emotional difficulties, and set therapeutic goals. Regular sessions with a mental health professional can offer structured support and ensure that individuals are progressing in their journey toward managing BPD effectively.

SELF-HELP BOOKS AND ONLINE RESOURCES

Self-help books and online resources offer valuable information and practical strategies for managing Borderline Personality Disorder.

Books authored by mental health professionals or individuals with lived experience provide insights into the disorder, coping techniques, and personal stories that can be both educational and inspiring. Reading these resources can help individuals better understand BPD and discover new strategies for managing symptoms.

Online resources, such as websites, blogs, and forums, offer accessible and often interactive content tailored to individuals with BPD. These platforms can include articles, videos, and downloadable materials that provide practical advice and self-help techniques. Many online resources also offer forums where individuals can connect with others, share experiences, and receive support from a wider community.

Utilizing online tools, such as mindfulness apps or mood-tracking software, can enhance self-management of BPD. These tools often offer features like guided meditation, mood journals, and progress tracking, which can support individuals in monitoring their symptoms and practicing self-care. Integrating these digital resources into daily routines can provide additional support and reinforce self-help strategies.

GOAL SETTING AND PERSONAL DEVELOPMENT

Goal setting and personal development are crucial for individuals with Borderline Personality Disorder as they provide direction and motivation. Setting specific, achievable goals helps individuals focus on positive changes and create a sense of purpose. Goals can range from improving self-care routines to developing new skills or addressing specific areas of emotional growth.

To effectively set and achieve goals, individuals should use the SMART criteria: Specific, Measurable, Achievable, Relevant, and Time-bound. For example, instead of a vague goal like "feel better," a SMART goal might be "practice mindfulness for 10 minutes daily for the next month." Breaking goals down into smaller, manageable steps makes them more attainable and allows individuals to track their progress and celebrate successes along the way.

Personal development activities, such as attending workshops, pursuing hobbies, or engaging in educational opportunities, can also support growth and self-improvement. These activities not only provide valuable skills and knowledge but also foster a sense of accomplishment and self-worth. By continuously working on personal development, individuals with BPD can build confidence and resilience, which enhances their overall quality of life.

CHAPTER SEVEN

MANAGING RELATIONSHIPS WITH BPD

NAVIGATING ROMANTIC RELATIONSHIPS

Navigating a romantic relationship when one partner has Borderline Personality Disorder (BPD) requires patience and understanding. Establishing a foundation of trust and consistent communication is vital. Begin by educating yourself about BPD to grasp the emotional fluctuations and behaviors associated with the disorder. This knowledge helps in responding to your partner's needs more effectively and empathetically. It is important to approach discussions with empathy, acknowledging their feelings without necessarily agreeing with their perceptions.

Creating a structured environment can provide stability for your partner. Routine and predictability in daily interactions help reduce the anxiety that often accompanies BPD.

Regular check-ins and open discussions about the relationship's progress can also reinforce security and prevent misunderstandings. Supportive behaviors, like validating emotions and encouraging therapy, further strengthen the bond and contribute to a healthier relationship dynamic.

Self-care for yourself is equally crucial. Being in a relationship with someone with BPD can be emotionally taxing, so maintaining your well-being should not be overlooked. Set aside time for activities that rejuvenates you and seeks support from friends, family, or a therapist. Balancing your needs with those of your partner ensures that you remain resilient and emotionally stable, which benefits the relationship overall.

COPING WITH FAMILY DYNAMICS

Coping with family dynamics involving a member with BPD involves setting clear and compassionate boundaries. It is essential to establish rules about acceptable behavior and communication to avoid triggering episodes. Discuss these boundaries openly and make sure they are consistent across interactions. This clarity helps family members understand the expectations and reduces the potential for conflict.

Regular family meetings or counseling sessions can be beneficial. These sessions provide a safe space to address issues, communicate openly, and work through conflicts with the guidance of a professional. Therapy can also aid in developing coping strategies tailored to the family's unique dynamics, promoting healthier interactions and mutual understanding.

Educate the family about BPD to foster empathy and reduce stigma. Knowledge about the disorder equips family members to support each other effectively and manage interactions more constructively.

Awareness and understanding of BPD can transform familial relationships, making them more supportive and less strained.

Handling interactions with a colleague or employee with BPD requires sensitivity and a strategic approach. Start by establishing professional boundaries to maintain a respectful and focused work environment. Clear communication about roles, expectations, and feedback helps in reducing misunderstandings and conflicts. It's important to be consistent and fair in your interactions, as unpredictability can exacerbate the challenges faced by someone with BPD.

Provide constructive feedback in a way that minimizes stress and anxiety. Use positive reinforcement and be specific about areas of improvement, ensuring that your feedback is balanced and supportive.

Being mindful of their emotional state and offering assistance or accommodations when necessary can also help in fostering a positive work environment.

Developing a supportive workplace culture can benefit everyone. Encouraging open dialogue, promoting mental health awareness, and offering resources such as employee assistance programs contribute to a more inclusive and understanding workplace. This approach not only supports those with BPD but also enhances overall team dynamics and productivity.

STRATEGIES FOR HEALTHY COMMUNICATION

Healthy communication with someone with BPD involves practicing active listening and validation. When engaging in conversations, focus on what the person is expressing and acknowledge their feelings without judgment. Reflective listening, where you restate their concerns to show understanding, helps in building trust and reducing misunderstandings.

Use clear, direct, and non-confrontational language. Avoid vague statements or passive-aggressive remarks, as these can lead to confusion and escalate emotions.

Be mindful of your tone and body language, ensuring they are calm and supportive. This approach helps in maintaining a constructive dialogue and preventing unnecessary conflict.

Encourage and model open communication by respectfully sharing your thoughts and feelings. Creating a safe space where both parties feel comfortable expressing themselves fosters mutual understanding and strengthens the relationship. Regularly check in on each other's needs and address any issues promptly to maintain healthy communication patterns.

SETTING BOUNDARIES AND EXPECTATIONS

Setting boundaries and expectations with someone with BPD is crucial for maintaining a balanced relationship. Clearly define what behaviors are acceptable and what are not, ensuring that these boundaries are communicated respectfully and consistently.

This clarity helps in preventing emotional upheaval and establishes a framework for interactions.

Be prepared to enforce these boundaries with firmness and compassion. Consistency in how boundaries are managed is key to their effectiveness. When boundaries are crossed, address the issue calmly and directly, reinforcing the agreed-upon limits while acknowledging the challenges faced by the person with BPD.

Establish mutual expectations for the relationship. Discuss and agree upon each person's needs and responsibilities, ensuring that both parties understand and accept these terms. Regularly revisit and adjust these expectations as needed to reflect any changes in the relationship or individual circumstances, promoting a healthy and adaptive dynamic.

CHAPTER EIGHT

CRISIS MANAGEMENT AND SAFETY PLANNING

IDENTIFYING WARNING SIGNS

Recognizing the early warning signs of Borderline Personality Disorder (BPD) is crucial for effective crisis management. Key indicators include sudden and intense emotional shifts, chronic feelings of emptiness, and difficulties in maintaining stable relationships. Individuals with BPD may exhibit impulsive behavior and a heightened sensitivity to perceived abandonment. Understanding these signs allows for timely intervention and support, potentially mitigating the severity of a crisis.

It's essential to be observant of behaviors such as self-harm, suicidal thoughts, or threats, as these can indicate a severe crisis phase. Additionally, fluctuations in mood and erratic decision-making can signal the need for immediate attention. Keeping a record of these behaviors can help in identifying patterns and understanding triggers, which is critical for developing a personalized crisis management plan.

Regular communication and validation of the person's feelings can provide insights into their emotional state. Engaging in open dialogues and creating a safe space for them to express their thoughts and feelings is key.

This proactive approach helps in spotting early warning signs and facilitates prompt action, reducing the likelihood of an escalation.

DEVELOPING A CRISIS PLAN

Creating a comprehensive crisis plan involves outlining specific steps to manage acute episodes of BPD. Begin by detailing emergency contact information, including mental health professionals, support groups, and trusted individuals who can offer immediate assistance. Establish clear protocols for what actions should be taken if warning signs are detected, including the preferred methods of communication and intervention.

The plan should include strategies for de-escalation, such as calming techniques and behavioral interventions that can be used during a crisis. It's also beneficial to outline the person's coping mechanisms and preferences for managing distress.

This personalized approach ensures that the plan is relevant and effective in addressing the individual's unique needs and triggers.

Regularly reviewing and updating the crisis plan is crucial to ensure its effectiveness. As circumstances and needs evolve, the plan should be adjusted accordingly.

Involve the individual with BPD in this process to enhance their engagement and adherence to the plan, fostering a collaborative approach to crisis management.

In situations where the risk of self-harm or severe emotional distress is imminent, seeking emergency help is paramount. Contacting emergency services or a mental health crisis hotline provides immediate support and intervention. Ensure that emergency contacts are clearly listed in the crisis plan and easily accessible in times of need.

Provide clear and concise information about the individual's condition and current crisis when reaching out for help. This includes describing the nature of the crisis, any immediate risks, and any relevant medical or psychological history. Effective communication ensures that emergency responders can offer the appropriate level of care and support.

It's important to have a plan for follow-up care after the initial crisis has been addressed. This may involve scheduling appointments with mental health professionals, arranging for continued support, and monitoring the individual's recovery process.

Coordinating with healthcare providers ensures that the person receives ongoing care and reduces the risk of future crises.

SAFETY TECHNIQUES AND COPING MECHANISMS

Implementing safety techniques and coping mechanisms is essential in managing BPD symptoms and preventing crises. Techniques such as grounding exercises, mindfulness practices, and cognitive-behavioral strategies can help individuals manage intense emotions and reduce impulsive behavior. Engaging in these practices regularly can enhance emotional resilience and provide practical tools for coping during difficult times.

Developing a personalized list of coping mechanisms, such as engaging in hobbies, physical activities, or relaxation techniques, can offer additional support. These activities should be tailored to the individual's preferences and interests, ensuring that they are both enjoyable and effective.

Encouraging the use of these techniques during periods of stress can aid in maintaining emotional stability.

Creating a structured daily routine that includes time for self-care, social interaction, and relaxation can also contribute to overall well-being. Consistent routines provide a sense of stability and predictability, which can be particularly beneficial for individuals with BPD. Regularly practicing these techniques and integrating them into daily life can help manage symptoms and prevent the escalation of crises.

SUPPORT RESOURCES FOR CRISIS SITUATIONS

Accessing support resources is a vital component of managing crises associated with BPD. Mental health organizations, support groups, and online communities offer valuable resources and emotional support. Connecting with these resources provides individuals and their families with additional guidance and reassurance during challenging times.

Utilizing crisis intervention services, such as hotlines and counseling services, can offer immediate support and practical advice. These services are often available 24/7 and can provide crucial assistance in times of need. Keeping contact information for these resources readily available ensures quick access when a crisis arises.

Engaging in community support networks and seeking out educational resources on BPD can also be beneficial. These resources offer insight into managing the disorder, coping strategies, and personal experiences from others who have faced similar challenges. Building a support network and staying informed can enhance overall crisis management and support.

CHAPTER NINE

LONG-TERM MANAGEMENT AND RECOVERY

SETTING AND ACHIEVING PERSONAL GOALS

Setting and achieving personal goals is essential for individuals managing Borderline Personality Disorder (BPD). Start by identifying clear, specific, and realistic goals that align with personal values and long-term aspirations.

Goals could range from improving interpersonal relationships to developing coping skills. Break these goals into smaller, manageable steps, making them less overwhelming and easier to track. For instance, if the goal is to enhance emotional regulation, a small step could be practicing mindfulness exercises daily.

Develop a structured plan that includes timelines and milestones to monitor progress. Using tools like journals or apps can help in tracking daily achievements and maintaining motivation. Regularly review and adjust the goals as needed based on personal growth and changing circumstances. For example, if a goal related to reducing impulsive behaviors shows significant progress, the focus might shift towards more advanced emotional regulation strategies.

Celebrate accomplishments and progress to reinforce positive behavior. Recognize and reward yourself for reaching milestones, which can boost self-esteem and encourage continued effort. Engage in activities that are enjoyable and affirming to maintain a positive outlook. By setting realistic goals and systematically working towards them, individuals with BPD can experience a sense of achievement and improve their overall well-being.

MONITORING PROGRESS AND ADJUSTING TREATMENT

Monitoring progress and adjusting treatment is a crucial part of managing BPD effectively. Start by keeping detailed records of symptoms, behaviors, and responses to treatment. Regular self-assessments and feedback from mental health professionals help in evaluating the effectiveness of the current treatment plan. Use standardized tools or questionnaires to gauge changes in mood, emotional regulation, and interpersonal relationships.

Based on the gathered data, make necessary adjustments to the treatment plan in collaboration with a healthcare provider. This may include altering medication dosages, exploring new therapeutic techniques, or adjusting therapy goals. For example, if a particular medication is causing unwanted side effects, discussing alternatives with a provider can help in finding a more suitable option.

Review progress regularly through scheduled appointments and self-monitoring activities. Adjustments should be made as needed to ensure that the treatment remains effective and aligned with the individual's evolving needs. Continuous evaluation helps in staying on track and making informed decisions about ongoing care, ultimately leading to better management of BPD.

BUILDING A SUPPORTIVE ENVIRONMENT

Building a supportive environment is essential for individuals with BPD to thrive. Start by fostering open communication with family, friends, and colleagues. Educate those around you about BPD to create understanding and empathy, which can lead to more supportive interactions. For instance, sharing information about BPD and its challenges can help loved ones offer more effective support.

Create a safe and positive space where emotional expression is encouraged and respected. Establish boundaries and ensure that the environment is free from triggers that may exacerbate symptoms. Engaging in supportive activities, such as group therapy or support groups, can also provide a sense of community and belonging.

Regularly assess and reinforce the support network to ensure it remains effective. Seek feedback from trusted individuals about how they can better support your needs and adjust the environment as necessary. Building and maintaining a supportive environment helps in managing BPD and fosters a sense of stability and security.

ADDRESSING RELAPSE AND SETBACKS

Addressing relapse and setbacks is an integral part of managing BPD. Begin by recognizing that setbacks are a natural part of the recovery process and should be addressed without self-blame. When experiencing a relapse, promptly identify the triggers and factors that contributed to the setback. Document these occurrences to understand patterns and prepare for future challenges.

Develop a proactive plan to address relapses, including strategies for immediate intervention and long-term prevention. This could involve revisiting coping skills, adjusting treatment plans, or seeking additional support. For example, if a specific stressor leads to a relapse, work with a therapist to develop strategies to manage that stressor effectively.

Use setbacks as learning opportunities to enhance resilience and strengthen coping mechanisms. Regularly review and refine personal goals and treatment

ENCOURAGING ONGOING THERAPY AND SUPPORT

Encouraging ongoing therapy and support is vital for the long-term management of BPD. Commit to attending regular therapy sessions and actively participating in the therapeutic process. Choose a therapy approach that resonates with personal needs, such as Dialectical Behavior Therapy (DBT) or Cognitive Behavioral Therapy (CBT), and adhere to the treatment plan. Consistent therapy helps in developing coping skills and addressing underlying issues.

Seek out additional support resources, such as support groups or online communities, to complement therapy. Engaging with others who have similar experiences can provide valuable insights and emotional support.

CHAPTER TEN

COMMON CONCERNS AND DETAILED FAQS

WHAT IS BORDERLINE PERSONALITY DISORDER (BPD)?

Borderline Personality Disorder (BPD) is a mental health condition characterized by a pervasive pattern of instability in mood, self-image, and interpersonal relationships. Individuals with BPD often experience intense and fluctuating emotions, leading to impulsive behaviors and difficulties in maintaining stable relationships. They may struggle with a chronic sense of emptiness, fear of abandonment, and difficulty regulating their emotions, which can result in self-harming behaviors or suicidal thoughts.

The disorder typically manifests during late adolescence or early adulthood, with symptoms that can be severe and affect various aspects of daily life. Common signs include extreme emotional reactions, difficulty managing anger, and a pattern of unstable relationships.

These symptoms often lead to significant distress and impairment in personal and professional life, requiring a comprehensive approach to treatment and support.

BPD is a complex condition, and its symptoms can overlap with other mental health disorders, making it essential to understand its unique characteristics. Effective management of BPD involves recognizing the specific challenges associated with the disorder and seeking appropriate interventions to address its multifaceted nature.

Diagnosing Borderline Personality Disorder involves a thorough assessment by a mental health professional, typically a psychologist or psychiatrist. The diagnostic process includes a detailed clinical interview where the clinician evaluates the individual's symptoms, history, and behavior patterns.

This assessment is often supplemented by standardized diagnostic tools and questionnaires to ensure a comprehensive evaluation.

During the diagnostic process, the clinician will look for specific criteria outlined in the Diagnostic and Statistical Manual of Mental Disorders (DSM-5), which includes patterns of unstable relationships, self-image, and mood. A diagnosis of BPD requires that these symptoms are persistent and cause significant distress or impairment in functioning. The clinician must differentiate BPD from other mental health conditions that may present with similar symptoms.

The diagnostic process also includes ruling out other potential causes of the symptoms, such as substance abuse or medical conditions, which could mimic or exacerbate BPD symptoms. This thorough evaluation helps ensure an accurate diagnosis and the development of an effective treatment plan tailored to the individual's needs.

WHAT ARE THE TREATMENT OPTIONS FOR BPD?

Treatment for Borderline Personality Disorder typically involves a combination of psychotherapy, medication, and support services. Psychotherapy, particularly Dialectical Behavior Therapy (DBT), is often considered the primary treatment approach. DBT focuses on helping individuals develop skills to manage emotions, improve interpersonal relationships, and reduce self-destructive behaviors. Other therapeutic approaches, such as Cognitive

Behavioral Therapy (CBT) and mentalization-based therapy, may also be beneficial depending on the individual's specific needs.

Medication may be prescribed to address specific symptoms associated with BPD, such as depression, anxiety, or mood swings. While there is no medication specifically approved for BPD, psychiatric medications can help manage co-occurring symptoms and improve overall functioning.

Individuals need to work closely with their healthcare provider to find the most effective medication regimen.

In addition to therapy and medication, support services such as group therapy and community support programs can play a crucial role in the treatment process. These services provide individuals with opportunities to connect with others who have similar experiences, share coping strategies, and build a support network that can enhance their overall well-being.

HOW CAN INDIVIDUALS WITH BPD MANAGE THEIR SYMPTOMS?

Individuals with Borderline Personality Disorder can manage their symptoms through various strategies and techniques that complement their treatment plan. Developing a strong therapeutic relationship with a mental health professional is crucial, as it provides a foundation for building trust and working through challenges.

Engaging in regular therapy sessions and applying the skills learned in therapy can help individuals manage their emotions and reduce impulsive behaviors.

Practicing self-care and mindfulness techniques can also be beneficial in managing BPD symptoms. Mindfulness practices, such as meditation and deep breathing exercises, can help individuals become more aware of their emotional states and develop healthier responses to stress. Establishing a routine, setting realistic goals, and practicing self-compassion can contribute to emotional stability and overall well-being.

Building a strong support system is essential for individuals with BPD. Connecting with supportive friends, family members, and peer support groups can provide encouragement and understanding. Effective communication and setting boundaries within relationships can also help manage interpersonal challenges and reduce the risk of conflict or emotional distress.

WHAT RESOURCES ARE AVAILABLE FOR PEOPLE WITH BPD?

There are numerous resources available for individuals with Borderline Personality Disorder to support their journey towards recovery and stability. Mental health organizations, such as the National Alliance on Mental Illness (NAMI) and the Borderline Personality Disorder Resource Center, offer valuable information, support groups, and educational materials tailored to individuals with BPD and their families.

Online communities and forums can provide a sense of connection and support, allowing individuals to share their experiences and learn from others facing similar challenges. Websites and apps dedicated to mental health and wellness often offer resources such as self-help tools, mindfulness exercises, and educational content about BPD.

Local mental health clinics and community health centers may offer specialized programs and services for individuals with BPD, including therapy, support groups, and crisis intervention. Individuals need to explore and utilize these resources to build a comprehensive support system that addresses their unique needs and promotes ongoing recovery and growth.